Favorite APPLIQUE PATTERNS

Favorite Applique Quilt Patterns from The Old Country Store

Favorite
APPLIQUE
PATTERNS

Favorite Applique Quilt Patterns from The Old Country Store

Volume
3

Designs by
Cheryl A. Benner
Text by
Rachel T. Pellman

Good Books®
Intercourse, PA 17534

Acknowledgments

Design by Cheryl A. Benner
Author photo by Kenneth Pellman

Favorite Applique Patterns
© 1992 by Good Books, Intercourse, PA 17534-0419
International Standard Book Number:
Volume 3-1-56148-075-4

Library of Congress Cataloging-in-Publication Data

Benner, Cheryl A., 1962—
    Favorite applique patterns from the Old Country Store /
design by Cheryl A. Benner : text by Rachel T. Pellman.
    p.   cm.

ISBN 1-56148-073-8 (pbk. : v. 1) : $15.95. — ISBN 1-56148-074-6
(pbk. : v. 2) : $15.95. — ISBN 1-56148-075-4 (pbk. : v. 3) : $15.95

    1. Appliqué—Patterns.   2. Quilting—Patterns.   I. Pell-
man, Rachel T. (Rachel Thomas)   II. Old Country Store (Intercourse, Pa.)   III. Title.
TT779.B44   1992   746.9'7—dc20   92-30871
                                                  CIP

Table of Contents

How to Begin
Preparing Background Fabric
Making Templates
Appliqueing
Assembling the Applique Quilt Top
Quilting on Applique Quilts
Marking Quilting Designs
Quilting
Binding
To Display Quilts
Other Projects
Signing and Dating Quilts

Patterns

Summer Bouquet

Fruit Wreath

Oriental Lily

Bridal Wreath

Straw Hat

Berry Basket

Bleeding Heart Swirl

Daisy Duck

Ewes Really Country

Mayflower

Summer Love

In Grandma's Garden

Ladybug

Strawberry Wreath

Old Country Tulip

Wedding Day

Mountain Lilies

Spring Bloomer

Garden Dance

Garden Treasure

Solitary Rose

Old Fashioned Bear

Bleeding Heart

Horn of Plenty

Tools of the Trade

Country Rooster

About The Old Country Store
About the Authors

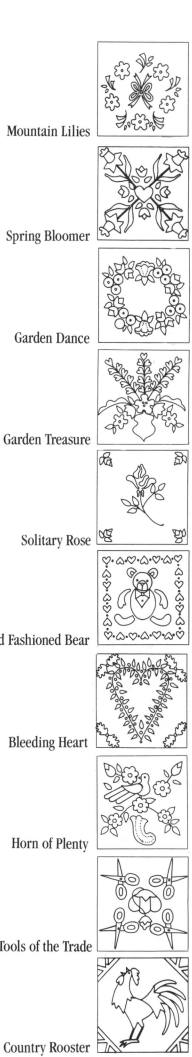

How to Begin

Read the following instructions thoroughly before beginning work on your quilt.

Wash all fabrics before cutting them. This process will both pre-shrink and test them for colorfastness. If the fabric is not colorfast after one washing, repeat the washings until the water remains clear or replace the cloth with another fabric. If fabrics are wrinkled after washing and drying, iron them before using them.

Fabrics suitable for quilting are generally lightweight, tightly woven cotton and cotton/polyester blends. They should not unravel easily and should not hold excessive wrinkles when squeezed and released. Because of the hours of time required to make a quilt, it is worth investing in high quality fabrics.

Fabric requirements given here are for standard 45″ wide fabric. If you use wider or more narrow fabrics, calculate the variations you will need.

All seams are sewn using ¼″ seam allowances. Measurements given include seam allowances except for applique pieces. (See "How to Applique" section.)

Preparing the Background Fabric

When purchasing fabric to be used for background and borders, it is best to buy the total amount needed from one bolt of fabric. This will assure that all the patches and borders will be the same shade. Dye lots can vary significantly from bolt to bolt of fabrics, and those differences are emphasized when placed next to each other in a quilt top.

Cutting diagrams are shown to make the most efficient use of fabric. Label each piece after it is cut. Mark right and wrong sides of fabric as well.

All applique designs are made to fit within a 20 inch finished square. These squares may be set together as blocks or tipped on their sides and filled in with triangles. Both options are shown and each gives patch sizes and fabric requirements. Applique designs are given as half of the total patch. The center point of each pattern is marked. To trace the applique design onto the fabric, mark the center of the fabric and align it with the center of the applique pattern. Trace the applique design lightly onto the right side of the fabric. Flop the pattern, again placing the center of the fabric over the center of the applique design and complete the design by tracing the second half. These placement lines will indicate where the pieces to be appliqued should be positioned.

Even though the applique pieces will be laid over these markings and stitched in place, it is important to mark these lines as lightly as possible.

A double or queen size quilt will require nine applique blocks if set straight together or five applique blocks filled in with triangles. If you want additional applique on the pillow throw section, adapt motifs from the square patch format to create a more elongated design across the pillow throw. Center the applique from side to side, but place it nearer the top of the quilt so there is extra fullness for tucking the quilt under the pillows. The space from the top of the pillow throw section to the highest point of the applique design should measure about 10 inches.

Making Templates

Make templates from patterns printed in this book, using material that will not wear along the edges from repeated tracing. Cardboard is suitable for pieces being traced only a few times. Plastic lids or the sides of plastic cartons work well for templates that will be used repeatedly. Quilt supply shops and art supply stores carry sheets of plastic that work well for template-making.

Quiltmaking demands precision. Remember that as you begin marking. Make applique templates in actual size without seam allowances. Test the template you have made against the original printed pattern for accuracy. Trace templates on the right side of the fabric, but spaced far enough apart so that you can cut them approximately ¼″ outside the marked line. The traced line is the fold line indicating the exact shape and finished edge of the applique piece. Since these lines will be on the right side of the fabric and will be on the folded edge, markings should be as light as possible.

Each applique piece needs to be traced separately (rather than having the fabric doubled) so the fold line is marked on each one. However, since some of the pieces face in opposite directions, half should be traced one way and the other half should be traced the opposite way.

Appliqueing

Begin by appliqueing the cut-out fabric pieces, one at a time, over the placement lines drawn onto the background fabric pieces. Be alert to the sequence in which the pieces are applied, so that sections which overlay each other are done in proper order. In cases where a portion of an applique piece is covered by another, the section being covered does not need to be stitched, since it will be held in place by the stitches on the section that overlays it.

Appliqueing is not difficult, but it does require patience and precision. The best applique work has perfectly smooth curves and sharply defined points. To achieve this, stitches must be very small and tight. First, pin the piece being appliqued to the outline on the background piece. Using thread that matches the piece being applied, stitch the piece to the background section, folding the seam allowance under the traced line on the applique piece. Fold under only a tiny section at a time. Very small pieces may require that the seam allowance be trimmed to less than ¼" so it can be folded under with less bulk.

The applique stitch is a running stitch going through the background fabric and emerging to catch only a few threads of the appliqued piece along the folded line. The needle should re-enter the background piece for the next stitch at almost the same place it emerged, creating a stitch so small that it is almost invisible along the edge of the appliqued piece. Stitches on the underside of the background fabric should be ¹⁄₁₆"–⅛" long.

To form sharp points, fold in one side and stitch almost to the end of the point. Fold in the opposite side to form the point and push the excess seam allowance under with the point of the needle. Excess seam allowance may be trimmed to eliminate bulk. Stitch tightly.

To form smooth curves, clip along the curves to the fold line. Fold under while stitching, using the needle to push under the seam allowances.

Commercially produced bias tape (¼ or ½ inch) can be used for vines and stems. This tape already has edges folded under and is convenient for appliqueing. Following appliqueing, you will need to embroider stems and vines that are too narrow for bias tape, eyes and beaks on birds, and small details on flowers.

Assembling the Appliqued Quilt Top

When all applique work is completed, the patches are ready to be assembled. See Cutting lay-out diagrams.

Quilting on Applique Quilts

Marking Quilting Designs

Quilting designs are marked on the surface of the quilt top. A lead pencil provides a thin line and, if used with very little pressure, creates markings that are easily seen for quilting, yet do not distract when quilting is completed. There are numerous marking pencils on the market, as well as chalk markers. Test whatever you choose on a scrap of fabric to be sure it performs as promised. Remember, quilting designs are not covered by quilting stitches, so the lines should be light or removable.

Outline quilting done close to applique work will highlight the applique and give it some dimension. Open space between applique work can be filled with straight line quilting diamonds for a complimentary quilting design. There are numerous templates available in quilt shops to fill open spaces and borders with anything from the most simple to ornate quilting motifs.

Quilting

A quilt consists of three layers—the back or underside of the quilt, the batting, and the top, which is the appliqued or patchwork layer. Quilting stitches follow a decorative pattern, piercing through all three layers of the quilt "sandwich" and holding it together.

Many quilters prefer to stretch their quilts into large quilting frames. These are built so that the finished area of the quilt can be rolled up as work on it progresses. This type of frame allows space for several quilters to work on the same quilt and is used at quilting bees. Smaller hoops can also be used to quilt small sections at a time. If you use one of these smaller frames, it is important that the three layers of the quilt be stretched and thoroughly basted to keep the layers together without puckering.

The quilting stitch is a simple running stitch. Quilting needles are called "betweens" and are shorter than "sharps," which are regular hand sewing needles. The higher the number, the smaller the needle. Many quilters prefer a size 8 or 9 needle.

Quilting is done with a single strand of quilting thread. The thread is knotted and the needle is inserted through the top layer about one inch away from the point where quilting will begin emerging on a marked quilting line. The knot is then gently tugged through the fabric so it is hidden between the layers. The needle then re-enters the quilt top, going through all layers of the quilt.

The quilter's one hand remains under the quilt to feel when the needle has successfully penetrated all layers and to help guide the needle back up to the surface. The upper hand receives the needle and repeats the process. A series of as many as five stitches can be "stacked" on the needle before pulling the thread through. When working curves, fewer stitches can be stacked. Quilting stitches should be pulled taut but not so tight as to pucker the fabric. When the entire length of thread has been used, the stitching should be reinforced with a tiny backstitch. The needle is then reinserted in the top layer, pushed through for a long stitch, and then pulled out and clipped.

The goal in quilting is to have straight, even stitches that are of equal length on both the top and bottom of the quilt. This is best achieved with hours of practice.

Binding

The final stage in completing a quilt is the binding, which finishes the quilt's raw edge. When binding the edges of a scalloped quilt, it is best to cut the binding strips on the bias. This allows more flex and stretch around curves. To cut on the bias, cut the fabric at a 45° angle to the straight of grain. When binding a straight-edged quilt, it is not necessary to cut the fabric on the bias.

A double thickness of binding on the edge of the quilt gives it additional strength and durability. To create a double binding, cut the binding strips 4–4½″ wide. Sew strips together to form a continuous length of binding. For a scalloped-edge quilt, this length will need to equal the two lengths plus the bottom edge of the quilt. The upper edge is straight. For a straight-edge binding, there will be four separate lengths—one for each side, top and bottom. The two lengths on the side will need to have an additional 4″ to allow for covering the corners.

Fold binding strips in half lengthwise with wrong sides together. Pin binding to quilt, having raw edges of quilt top and raw edges of binding even. Stitch through all thicknesses (binding, quilt top, batting and quilt back). Sew top and bottom bindings on first. Attach sides, sewing over top of extended bindings on upper and lower edges.

To sew binding on a scalloped edge, baste the raw edges of the quilt together. Mark the scallops. Sew the binding along the marked edge. Trim the scallops even with the edge of the binding. Wrap the binding around to the back, enclosing the raw edges and covering the stitch line. Slipstitch in place with thread that matches the color of the binding fabric.

To Display Quilts

Wall quilts can be hung in various ways. One is simply to tack the quilt directly to the wall. However, this is potentially damaging to both quilt and wall. Except for a permanent hanging, this is probably not the best way.

Another option is to hang the quilt like a painting. To do this, make a narrow sleeve from matching fabric and hand-sew it to the upper edge of the quilt along the binding. Insert a dowel rod through the sleeve and hang the rod by wire or nylon string.

The quilt can also be hung on a frame. This method requires velcro or fabric to be attached to the frame itself. In the case of velcro, one side is stapled to the frame. The opposite velcro is hand-sewn on the edges of the quilt and attached carefully to the velcro on the frame. If fabric is attached to the frame, the quilt is then handstitched to the frame itself.

Quilts can also be mounted inside plexiglass by a professional framery. This method, often reserved for antique quilts, can provide an acid-free, dirt-free and, with special plexiglass, a sun-proof environment for your quilt.

Other Projects

These applique patterns are adaptable to other projects as well. To make a wallhanging, follow the instructions for appliqueing but use only one square patch. Add a border with decorative quilting and you have a lovely wallhanging. Borders on wallhangings may be mitered for a more tailored look.

Pillows can also be made using a single patch. Applique the pillow top and quilt the patch. To make the back of the pillow, cut a square equal in size to the front in either matching or contrasting fabric.

Make a ruffle using one of the fabrics used in the applique design. To make the ruffle, cut three strips of fabric measuring 4½″ x 45″ each. Sew these strips together to form a continuous length. Bring the two ends together, wrong sides together, and stitch to create a fabric circle. Fold the fabric circle in half, bringing top and bottom edges (and wrong sides) together. Stitch along the raw edge with a long running stitch the entire circumference of the circle. Gather the circle to fit around the edges of the quilted top. Pin the ruffle to the pillow top with the raw edges even and spread the gathers evenly throughout. Baste ruffle to pillow top.

With right sides together and ruffle sandwiched between the layers, pin back to pillow top. Stitch back to top through all layers, leaving a five-inch opening along one side. Trim seams. Turn pillow right side out. Stuff pillow with polyester fiberfill. Slipstitch opening.

Signing and Dating Quilts

To preserve history for future generations, sign and date the quilts you make. Include your initials and the year the quilt was made. This data is usually added rather discreetly in a corner of the quilt. It can be embroidered, or quilted among the quilting designs. Another alternative is to stitch or write the information on a separate piece of fabric and handstitch it to the back of the quilt. Whatever method you choose, this is an important part of finishing a quilt.

Cutting Layout for Queen-size Quilt

Final size—approximately 92" × 109"
Total yardage for quilt top—8⅞ yards
Total yardage for quilt back—6¼ yards
plus 12" left from cutting
borders on front.

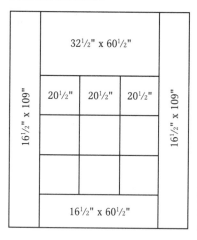

Side Borders
112" x 45" (3⅛ yards)

Side Border—16½"
Side Border—16½"
Quilt Back—12" left

Quilt Back (6¼ yards) plus 12" left
from cutting borders on front

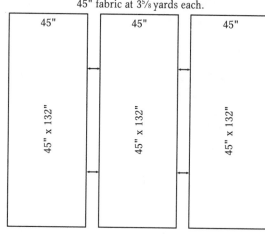

Patches, Bottom Border, Pillow throw (5¾ yards=207")

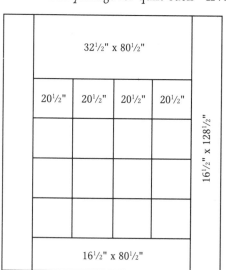

Cutting Layout for King-size Quilt

Final size—approximately 112" × 128"
Total yardage for quilt top
(Patches, border and Pillow throw)—12¾ yards
Total yardage for quilt back—11⅛ yards

Quilt Back (11⅛ yards) 3 sections of
45" fabric at 3⅝ yards each.

3⅝ yards=132"

Side Border—16½" x 128½"
Side Border—16½" x 128½"

Patches, Bottom Border, Pillow throw (9⅛ yards=328")

Alternate Layout
Cutting Layout for Queen-size or Double-Size Quilt

Final size—approximately 93" × 108"
Measurements include seam allowances

Total yardage for quilt top—8³/₈ yards
Total yardage for quilt back—6¹/₄ yards
plus 11" remaining from cutting
borders of quilt top.

A Patches—cut 5— 21¹/₂" square

B Corner Triangles— 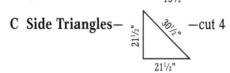 —cut 4

C Side Triangles— —cut 4

D Pillow Throw—32¹/₂" x 60¹/₂"
E Bottom Border—17" x 60¹/₂"
F Side Borders—17" x 109"

Triangular Patches (1¹/₈ yards)

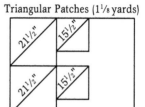

Side Borders (3¹/₈ yards)

| Side Borders—17" x 109" |
| Side Borders—17" x 109" |
| Quilt Back—11" left |

Square Patches, Bottom Border, Pillow Throw (4¹/₈ yards)

| | Bottom Border 17" x 60¹/₂" | 21¹/₂" |
| Pillow Throw 32¹/₂" x 60¹/₂" | 21¹/₂" 21¹/₂" 21¹/₂" 21¹/₂" | |

Quilt Back (6¹/₄ yards) plus 11" left from side border section of fabric

| 11" | 45" | 45" |
| 11" x 112" | 45" x 112" | 45" x 112" |

Assembly Instructions for Queen-size/Double-size

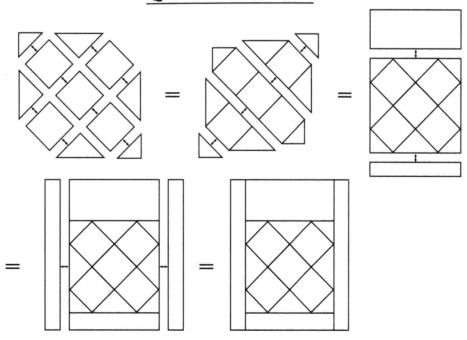

Fruit Wreath

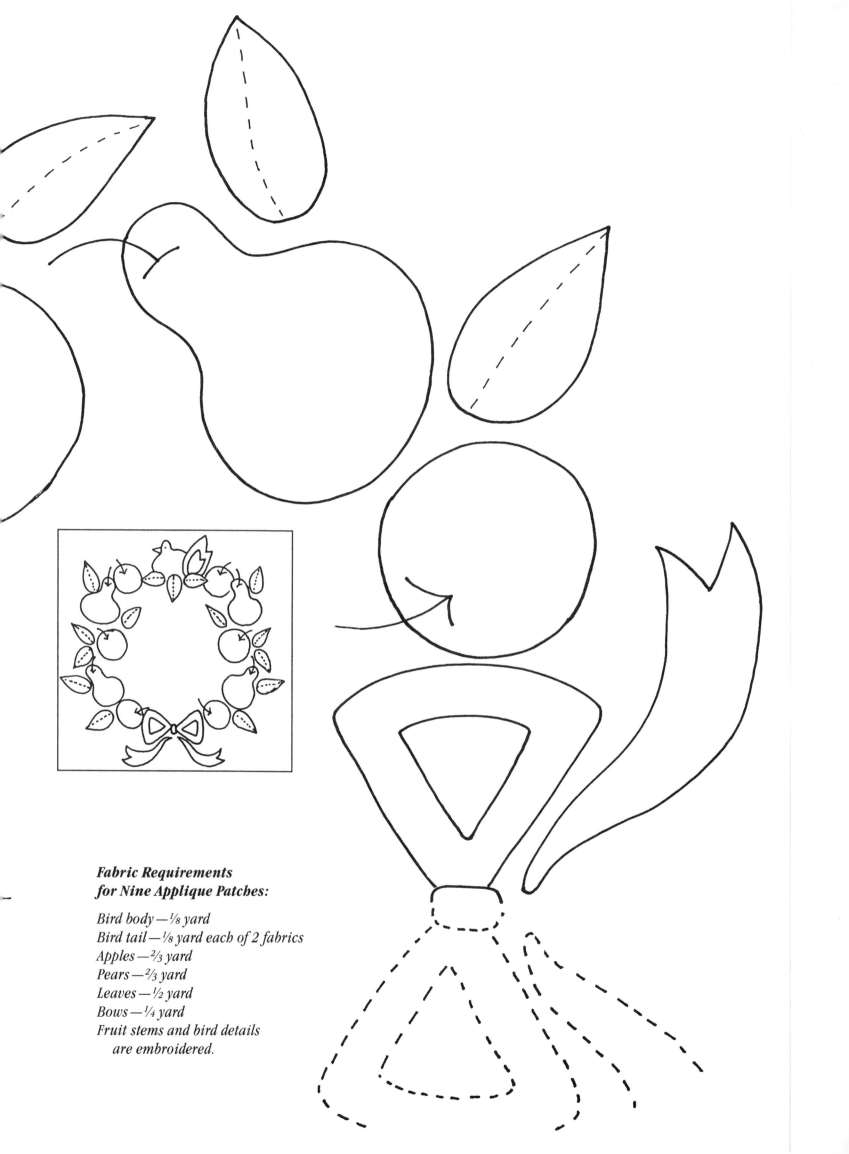

**Fabric Requirements
for Nine Applique Patches:**

Bird body—1/8 yard
Bird tail—1/8 yard each of 2 fabrics
Apples—2/3 yard
Pears—2/3 yard
Leaves—1/2 yard
Bows—1/4 yard
Fruit stems and bird details
    are embroidered.

Oriental Lily

**Fabric Requirements
for Nine Applique Patches:**

Lily base — ½ yard
Lily edge — ¼ yard
Lily back — ⅓ yard
Flower piston — ⅛ yard
Buds — ⅛ yard
Leaves — ¾ yard
Bias tape for stems — 15 yards

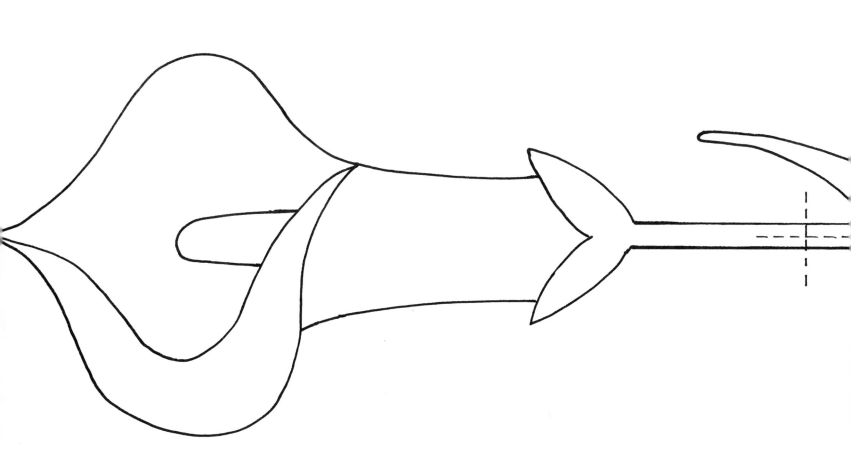

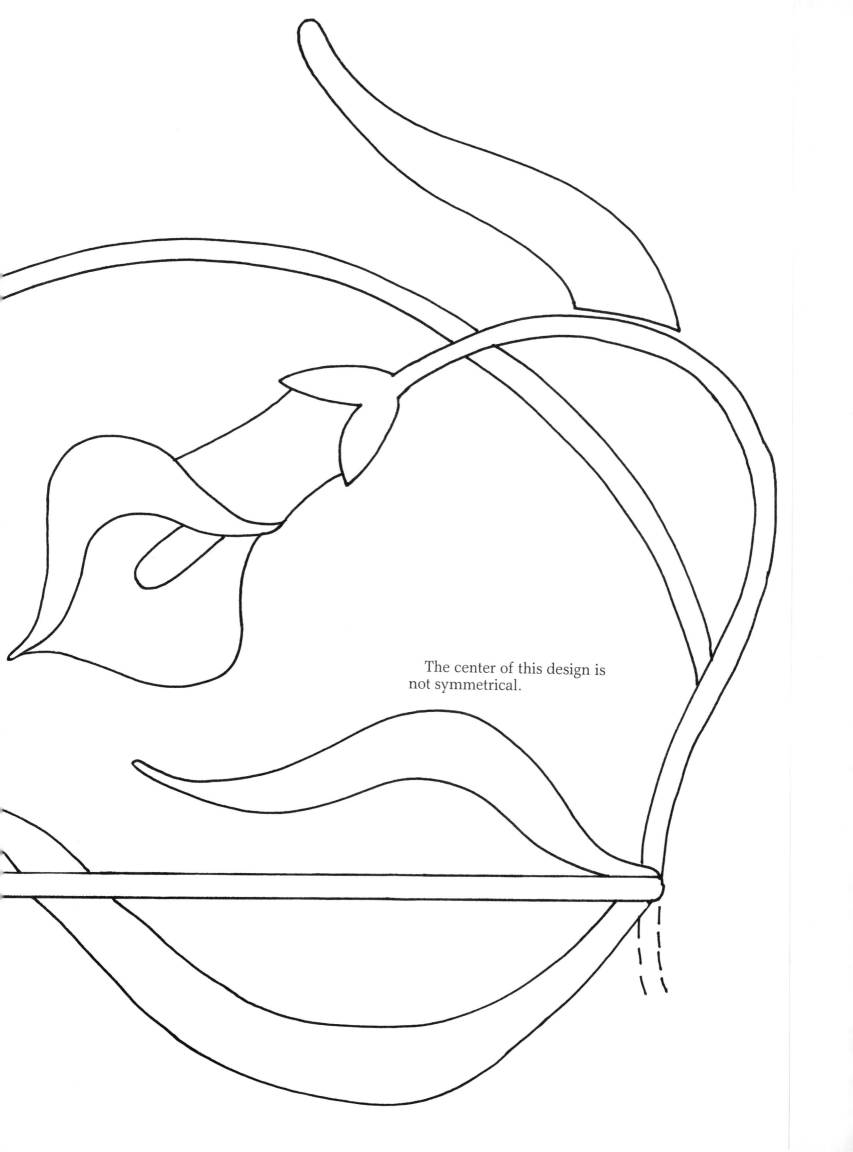

The center of this design is
not symmetrical.

Bridal Wreath

**Fabric Requirements
for Nine Applique Patches:**

Hearts — 1 yard
Leaves — 1½ yards
Bias tape for vine — 10½ yards

Heart appears in each of the
four corners.

Straw Hat

**Fabric Requirements
for Nine Applique Patches:**

Round flowers — 1/3 *yard each of 3
   fabrics*
Petal flowers — 1/4 *yard*
Leaves — 3/4 *yard*
Bows — 1/4 *yard*

Straw Hats — 1 1/4 *yard*
*Bias tape for hat
bands* — 4 1/2 *yards*

The other side of the Straw
hat does not have cluster of
flowers. Refer to diagram of
complete layout.

Berry Basket

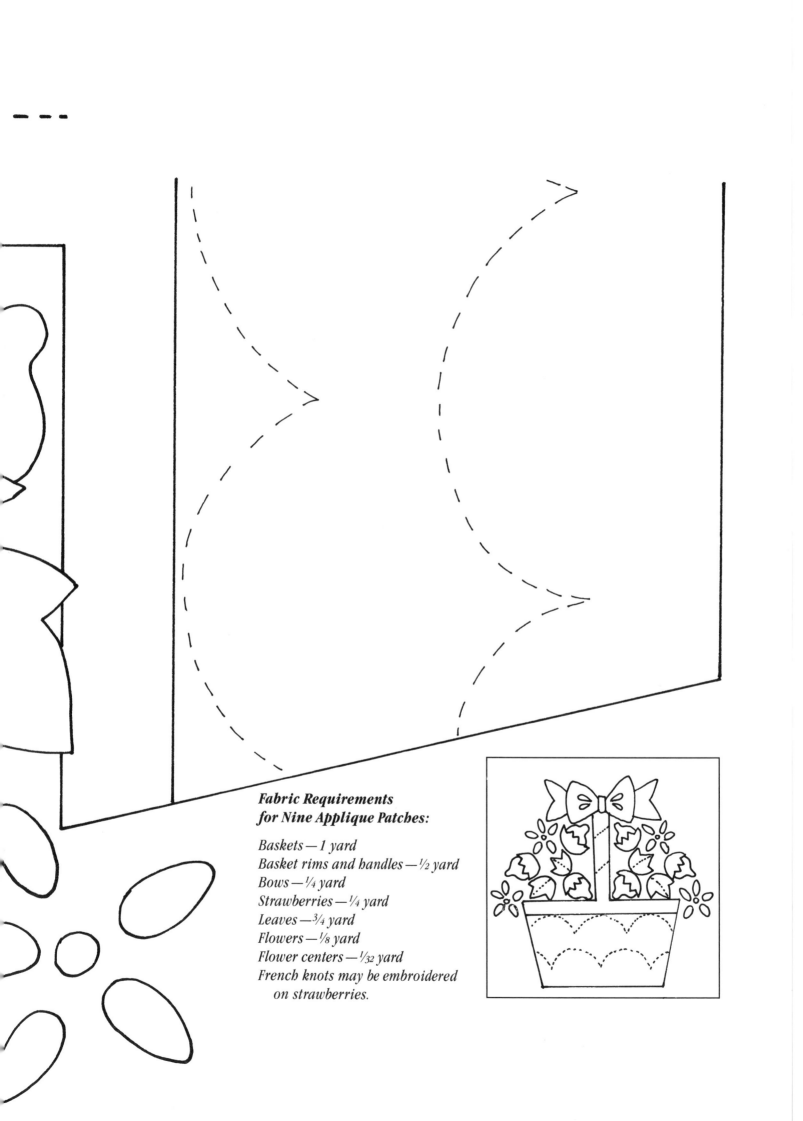

**Fabric Requirements
for Nine Applique Patches:**

Baskets — 1 yard
Basket rims and handles — ½ yard
Bows — ¼ yard
Strawberries — ¼ yard
Leaves — ¾ yard
Flowers — ⅛ yard
Flower centers — ¹⁄₃₂ yard
French knots may be embroidered
   on strawberries.

Bleeding Heart Swirl

Fabric Requirements
for Nine Applique Patches:

Hearts—¾ yard
Leaves—⅝ yard
Berries—⅛ yard
Bias tape for stems
and heart details—17 yards

Rotate design 180 degrees to
complete layout of patch.

Daisy Duck

**Fabric Requirements
for Nine Applique Patches:**

Duck body — ¼ yard
Duck wing — ⅛ yard
Duck feet — ⅛ yard
Duck beak — 1/16 yard
Hat — ⅛ yard
Bow — ⅛ yard
Flowers — 1/16 yard of 3 fabrics
Leaves — 1/16 yard
Umbrella — ½ yard
Umbrella handle — ⅛ yard
Details on duck may be embroidered.

Flop umbrella template to create the other half of the umbrella.

Embroider flower stem on Duck's hat. Add daisy on the end of the stem.

Ewes Really Country

**Fabric Requirements
for Nine Applique Patches:**

Sheep body — ⅛ *yard*
Sheep face and legs — ⅛ *yard*
Hearts — ⅛ *yard*
Leaves — ⅜ *yard*
Berries — ¼ *yard*

Heart and leaves appear
in each of the four corners.

Mayflower

Fabric Requirements
for Nine Applique Patches:

Background of center flower—½ yard
Round flowers—⅛ yard
Round flower centers—1/16 yard
Tulip sides—½ yard
Tulip centers—⅜ yard
Leaves—⅞ yard
Bias tape for stems—3 yards

Summer Love

**Fabric Requirements
for Nine Applique Patches:**

*Large flowers—½ yard
Flower centers—⅛ yard
Buds—¼ yard
Leaves—1 yard
Bias tape for stems—9 yards*

Quilt hearts.

In Grandma's Garden

**Fabric Requirements
for Nine Applique Patches:**

Five petal flowers—3/4 yard
Scalloped flowers—1/4 yard
Flower centers—1/8 yard
Leaves—1 yard
Bias tape for stems—11 1/2 yards

Ladybug

**Fabric Requirements
for Nine Applique Patches:**

Ladybug bodies—¼ yard
Ladybug spots and heads—¼ yard
Leaves—¼ yard
Flowers—½ yard
Hearts—⅛ yard
Bias tape for vines—36 yards

Use narrow bias tape to create winding wreath.

Strawberry Wreath

Fabric Requirements
for Nine Applique Patches:

Bows —½ yard
Flowers —¼ yard
Strawberries —½ yard
Leaves —¾ yard
French knots may be embroidered
   on strawberries.

Old Country Tulip

**Fabric Requirements
for Nine Applique Patches:**

Tulips — ⅔ yard
Hearts — ⅔ yard
Leaves — ⅝ yard
Bias tape for stems — 6 yards

Wedding Day

**Fabric Requirements
for Nine Applique Patches:**

Bird body — 1/3 yard
Bird wing — 1/8 yard
Bird tail — 1/16 yard each of 3 fabrics
Heart fans — 1/4 yard each of 3 fabrics
Flower petals — 3/8 yard
Flower centers — 1/4 yard
Bows — 1 1/3 yard
Leaves — 1/8 yard

Embroider eye as shown.

Mountain Lilies

**Fabric Requirements
for Nine Applique Patches:**

Bows—⅓ yard
Curved flowers—1 yard
Trumpet flowers—½ yard
Flower centers—⅛ yard
Leaves—⅛ yard

Quilt Bow with center.

Spring Bloomer

Fabric Requirements
for Nine Applique Patches:

Hearts—¼ yard
Daffodil base—⅔ yard
Daffodil center—⅜ yard
Daffodil top—¼ yard
Leaves—1 yard
Buds—⅛ yard
Bias tape for stems—7 yards

Garden Dance

Rotate template clockwise one half turn.

**Fabric Requirements
for Nine Applique Patches:**

Round flowers—½ yard
Round flower centers—¼ yard
Tulip side petals—⅜ yard
Tulip center petals—¼ yard
Tulip top—¼ yard
Buds—¼ yard
Leaves—1 yard

Garden Treasure

**Fabric Requirements
for Nine Applique Patches:**

Tear-shaped leaves—⅛ yard
Large leaves—½ yard
Rounded-edge flower—¾ yard
Pointed flower—¼ yard
Hearts—½ yard
Flower centers—¹⁄₁₆ yard

Quilting lines on large leaf
are random veins, to
resemble an actual leaf.

Solitary Rose

Fabric Requirements for Nine Applique Patches:

Flowers —¾ yard
Leaves — 1 yard
Stems are embroidered.

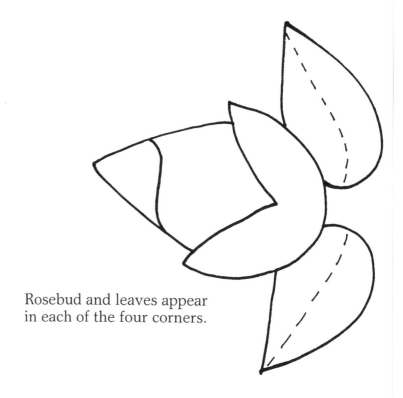

Rosebud and leaves appear
in each of the four corners.

Old Fashioned Bear

Fabric Requirements
for Nine Applique Patches:

Teddy body — 1¼ *yards*
Nose — ⅛ *yard*
Bow tie — ⅛ *yard*
Vest — ⅛ *yard*
Hearts — ⅞ *yard*
Dots — ⅛ *yard*
Facial details are embroidered.

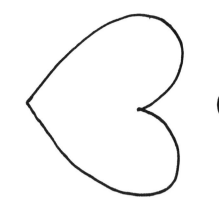

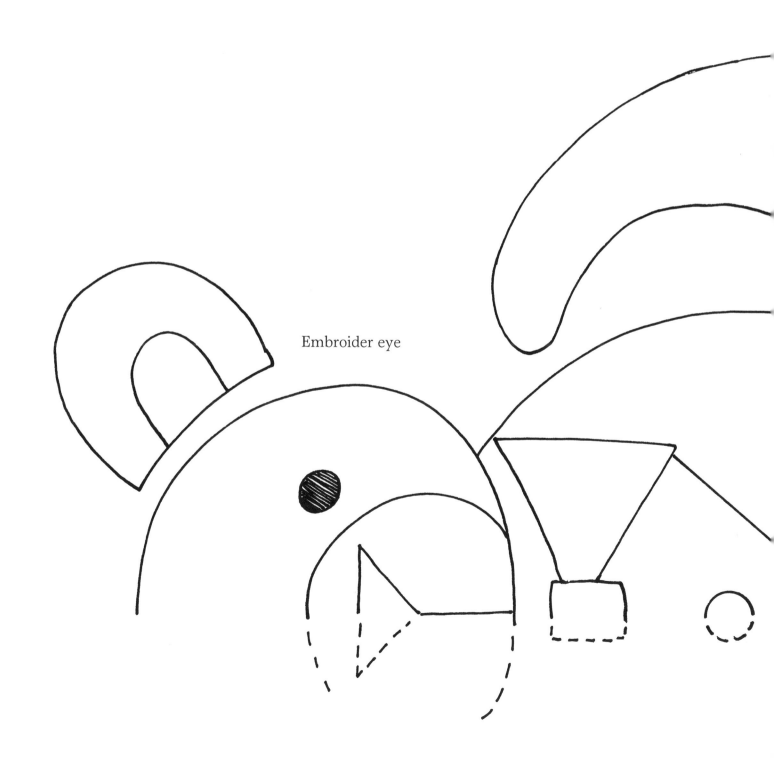

Embroider eye

Heart border continues
around entire patch.

Bleeding Heart

Leaf motif appears in each of the four corners.

**Fabric Requirements
for Nine Applique Patches:**

Oak leaves — 1/3 yard
Tear-shaped leaves — 1¾ yards
Berries — 1 yard
Bias tape for heart vine — 12 yards

Horn of Plenty

This pattern is not symmetrical. Refer to diagram of complete layout to see position of templates to create the other half.

Fabric Requirements for Nine Applique Patches:

Horn — 1/3 yard
Bird body — 1/4 yard
Bird wing — 1/4 yard
Bird tail — 1/3 yard
Flowers — 5/8 yard
Flower centers — 1/8 yard
Buds — 1/8 yard
Leaves — 1 yard
Vines and bird details are embroidered.

Tools of the Trade

**Fabric Requirements
for Nine Applique Patches:**

*Sewing cushions—⅓ yard each of
   3 fabrics
Scissors handles—⅜ yard
Scissors blades—⅜ yard
Vine on sewing cushion is embroidered. A button may be used for the
   scissors screw.*

Scissors appear in each of the
four corners.

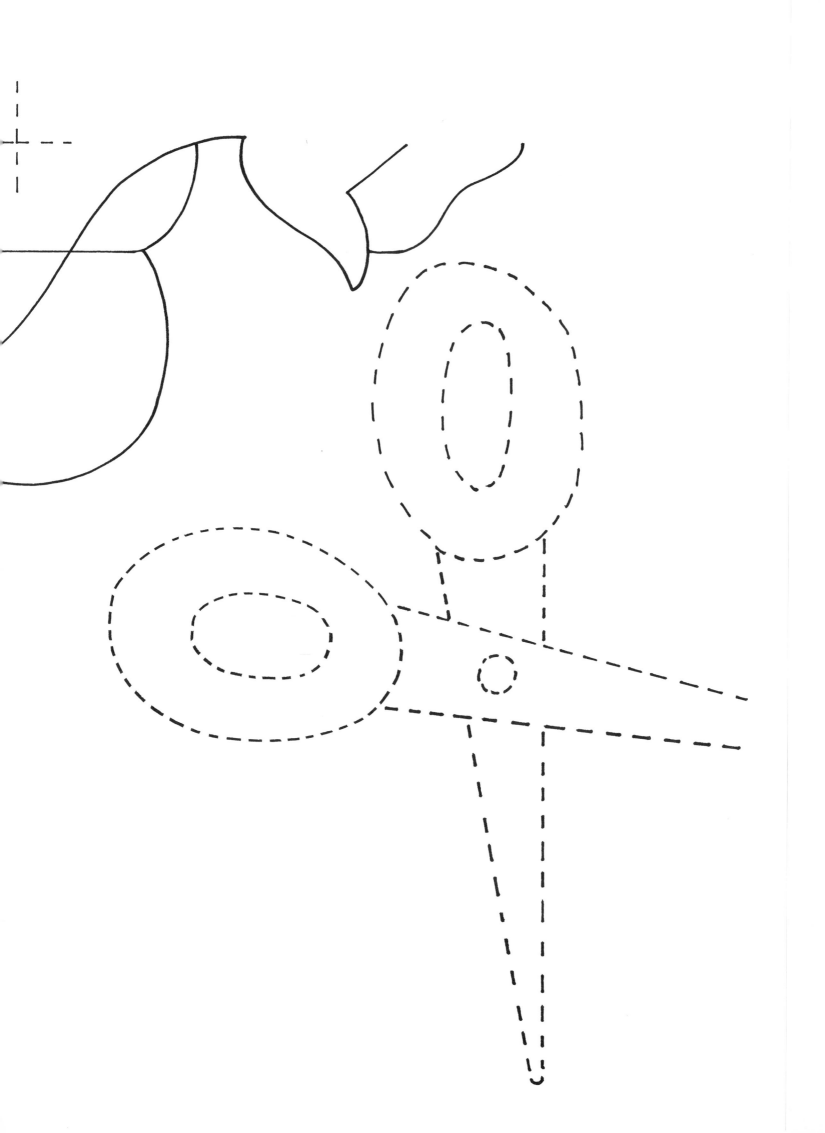

Country Rooster
Part One

2

Cut along dotted line.

Fabric Requirements for Nine Applique Patches:

Rooster body — ⅔ yard each of
   3 fabrics
Rooster tail feathers — ⅛ yard each
   of 5 fabrics
Rooster feet — ¼ yard
Rooster comb and waddle — ¼ yard
Corner bars — ⅞ yard
Rooster eye and beak are embroidered.

To complete layout, cut along dotted lines.
   Connect corresponding letters and notches and tape together.

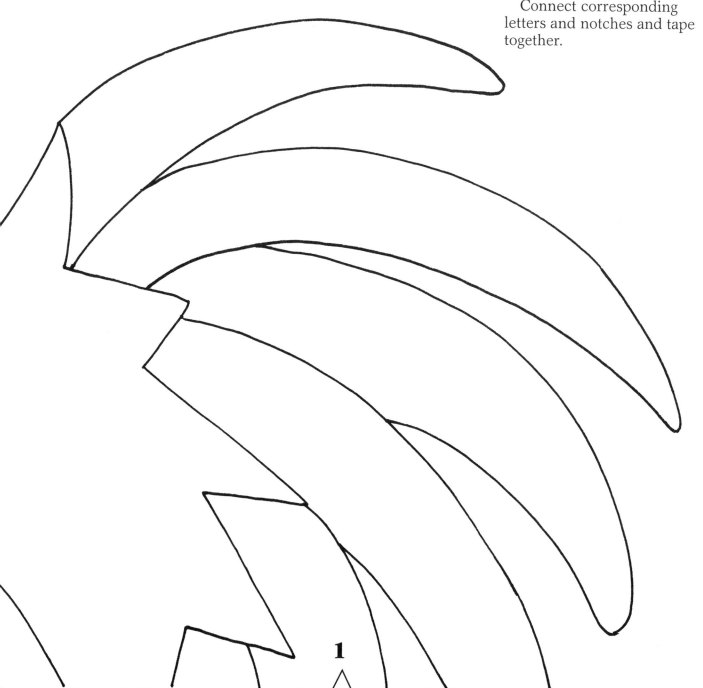

1

Cut along dotted line.

Country Rooster
Part Two

Cut along dotted line.

2

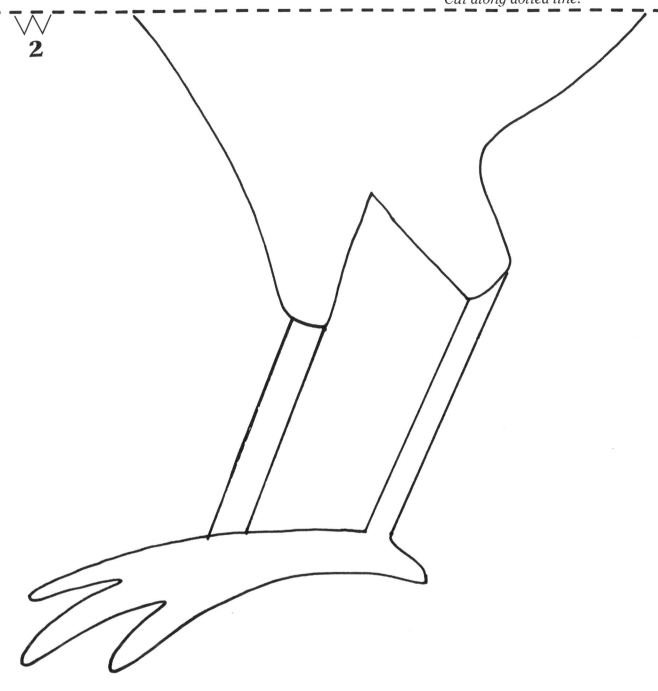

Cut along dotted line.

1

Order Form

(all books are paperback)

Quantity

_____ copies of *The Country Songbird Quilt* @ $12.95 each = $ _____

_____ copies of *The Country Lily Quilt* @ $12.95 each = $ _____

_____ copies of *The Country Love Quilt* @ $12.95 each = $ _____

_____ copies of *The Country Bride Quilt* @ $12.95 each = $ _____

_____ copies of *The Country Bride Quilt Collection* @ $12.95 each = $ _____

_____ copies of *The Country Paradise Quilt* @ $12.95 each = $ _____

_____ copies of *Country Quilts for Children* @ $12.95 each = $ _____

_____ copies of *Amish Quilt Patterns* @ $12.95 each = $ _____

_____ copies of *Small Amish Quilt Patterns* @ $12.95 each = $ _____

_____ copies of *Making Animal Quilts: Patterns and Projects* @ $12.95 each = $ _____

_____ copies of *Patterns for Making Amish Dolls and Doll Clothes* @ $12.95 each = $ _____

Subtotal $ _____

PA residents add 6% sales tax _____

Shipping and handling (Add 10%, $1.50 minimum) _____

TOTAL $ _____

METHOD OF PAYMENT

☐ Check or Money Order (payable to Good Books in U.S. funds)

☐ Please charge my:

    ☐ MasterCard   ☐ Visa

_____ _____ _____ _____ exp. date _____

Signature _____

Name _____

Name _____

Address _____

City _____ State or Province ____ Postal Code _____

Telephone (_____) _____

SHIP TO: (if different)

Name _____

Address _____

City _____ State or Province ____ Postal Code _____

Telephone (_____) _____

Mail order to **Good Books**, Main Street, P.O. Box 419, Intercourse, PA 17534-0419; Or call 1-800-762-7171 (in PA and Canada, call collect 717/768-7171).

(Prices subject to change without notice.)

About The Old Country Store

Cheryl A. Benner and Rachel T. Pellman are on the staff of The Old Country Store, located along Route 340 in Intercourse, Pennsylvania. The Store offers crafts from more than 300 artisans, most of whom are local Amish and Mennonites. There are quilts of traditional and contemporary designs, patchwork pillows and pillow kits, afghans, stuffed animals, dolls, tablecloths and Christmas tree ornaments. Other handcrafted items include potholders, sunbonnets and wooden toys.

For the do-it-yourself quilter, the Store offers quilt supplies, fabric at discount prices, and a large selection of quilt books and patterns.

Located on the second floor of the Store is The People's Place Quilt Museum. The Museum, which opened in 1988, features antique Amish quilts and crib quilts, as well as a small collection of dolls, doll quilts, socks and other decorative arts.

The People's Place Quilt Museum

The Old Country Store has a wide variety of fabrics. Our staff would be happy to color coordinate fabrics for any quilt pattern in this book. Let us know which quilt you are making and what colors you want to work with. We'll cut the appropriate amount of fabrics for the applique pieces and send them to you.

Call during Store hours (9am–5pm, Eastern time, Monday through Saturday), 717/768-7171.

About the Authors

Cheryl A. Benner and Rachel T. Pellman together developed the book *Favorite Applique Patterns from The Old Country Store.* Benner created the patterns; Pellman wrote the text. This is Benner's and Pellman's seventh collaboration on quilt designs with related books. Their earlier books are the popular *The Country Love Quilt, The Country Lily Quilt, The Country Songbird Quilt, The Country Bride Quilt Collection, The Country Paradise Quilt* and *Country Quilts for Children.*

Benner, her husband Lamar, and young son live in Honeybrook, PA. She is a graduate of the Art Institute of Philadelphia (PA). Benner is art director for Good Enterprises, Intercourse, PA.

Pellman lives near Lancaster, PA and is manager of The Old Country Store, Intercourse. She is co-author of *The Country Bride Quilt.* She is also the author of *Amish Quilt Patterns* and *Small Amish Quilt Patterns;* co-author with her husband, Kenneth, *of A Treasury of Amish Quilts, The World of Amish Quilts, Amish Crib Quilts, Amish Doll Quilts, Dolls and Other Playthings* and *A Treasury of Mennonite Quilts.*

The Pellmans are the parents of two sons.